Lazy Dog

carol fields brown

Illustrated by Yesenia A. Thomas

Lazy Dog

The Dramatic Pen Press

Lolo, Montana

ISBN 13: 978-0692631140

ISBN 10: 0692631143

Original Illustrations by Yesenia A. Thomas

Printed in the United States of America
2016—First Edition

www.TheDramaticPen.com

The heavens are telling the Glory of God.

Psalm 19:1

The quick brown fox jumps
over the lazy dog.

The strong black horse runs along the country lane.

The soft orange cat looks out from the paper bag.

The fat red squirrel climbs
around the sturdy oak.

The swift bright fish swims among the shiny stones.

The proud white goat
springs upon the junky car.

- -

- -

- -

The great blue whale leaps
out of the crashing sea.

The white striped skunk strolls
out on the picnic grounds.

The sleek black crow caws
high in the swaying pine.

The quiet gray mouse
peeps

around the wooden pail.

The slick pink pig sinks
into the oozy mud.

_____

- -

_____

- -

_____

- -

_____

The small green snake slides
under the mossy stone.

Can you write your own matching sentences?
Here is a chart to help you.

Article	adjective	adjective	noun subject	verb present tense	adverb/ preposition	article	adjective	noun/ object
1 syllable	1 syllable	1 syllable	1 syllable	1 syllable	2 syllables	1 syllable	2 syllables	1 syllable
The	quick	brown	fox	jumps	over	the	lazy	dog.

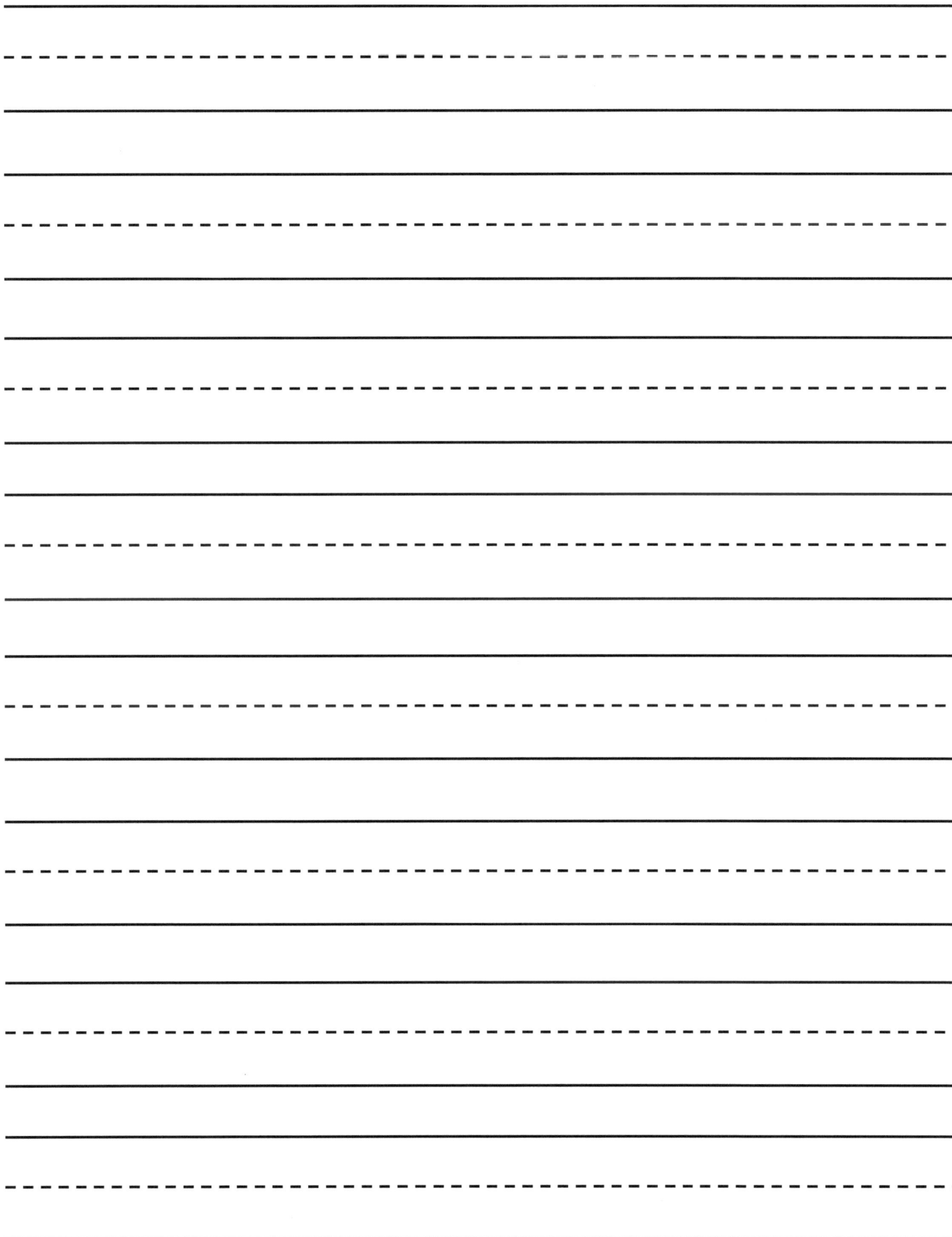

FIND NOVELS, NON-FICTION BOOKS, INTERACTIVE PARTY GAMES, CHILDREN'S BOOKS, POETRY, AND RELIGIOUS DRAMA AT:

www.TheDramaticPen.com

www.facebook.com/thedramaticpen

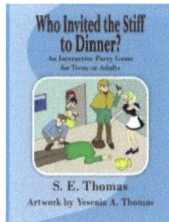

Who Invited the Stiff to Dinner?
An Interactive Mystery Party Game
for Teens or Adults

The guests have arrived for a distinguished dinner party at the wealthy English estate of Richard Orwell Mortice. But why would he invite so many of his enemies into his home, along with a Scotland Yard Inspector? When the maid discovers good ol' Rick O. Mortice dead, the Inspector and his overly eager Lieutenant are out to discover the culprit! Everyone has a motive and the accusations fly—but not before they go ahead and sit down to a luxurious meal. After all, why let one stiff ruin dinner? *(Requires 15 participants.)*

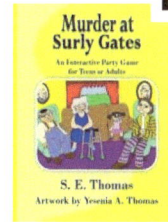

Murder at Surly Gates
An Interactive Mystery Party Game
for Teens or Adults

Tensions rise when the cantankerous residents of Surly Gates Nursing Home endure money-hungry relatives, a spoiled brat, and the child's incompetent mother during visitors' hours. When the nursing home manager turns up dead in his office, everyone is a suspect! Who had something to gain? What happened to Badger's heart pills? Why does Lily, a former beauty queen, still sway her hips behind her walker? Buster, a former security guard, and Doyle, a bumbling cop, want to solve this case! *(Requires 15 participants.)*

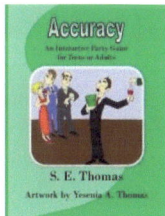

Accuracy
An Interactive Mystery Party Game
for Teens or Adults

A successful, though pompous, author is murdered on the night of his new book debut celebration. A note—intended to stop the murder—actually spurns the killer into action due to some rearranged punctuation. Who wrote the note? Who tampered with the note? Who carried out the false instructions? Nearly everyone has a motive! An intelligent, Spanish attorney with a very thick accent discovers the truth. *(Requires 11 participants.)*

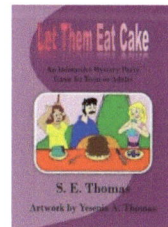

Let Them Eat Cake
An Interactive Mystery Party Game
for Teens or Adults

A reputable cake-baking contest is underway and the contestants are vying to win 20% of the stock in the wealthy contest sponsor's restaurant business. Then the sponsor turns up dead! He ate an entire cake ridden with arsenic-bearing apple seeds! Who gave him the cake? Who wanted him dead? Why in the world didn't he stop at the first bite? A bumbling security guard who is allergic to flour is on the case! *(Requires 14 participants.)*

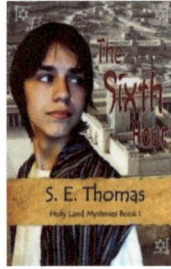

The Sixth Hour
Book I of the Holy Land Mysteries Series
By S. E. Thomas

Can Darash, a Jewish teenager, track a killer, rescue his family from ruin, and discover the truth about Yeshua? The rebel, Yeshua, drove the merchants and moneychangers from the Temple with a whip. Hours later, one of them was murdered. Now fifteen-year-old Darash must find a way to protect his family from poverty even as he struggles with the grief of losing his father. When another murder is committed, Darash finds himself searching for a dangerous killer and relying on an old, blind basket-weaver for help. Despite the odds, Darash discovers he has strength of character, a deep compassion for others, and an uncanny knack for problem-solving. But will he be able to expose the killer before the killer finds him? Available in paperback ($13.95) or eBook ($5.99 from Kindle or Nook.)

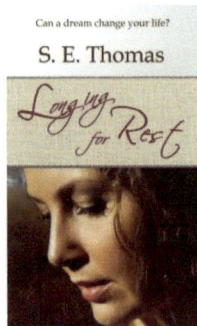

The Scrolls of the Nevi'im Series
The prophets of the Old Testament come alive with...

Book I: Habakkuk's Plea: A Prophet of Elohim
Book II: Habakkuk's Plea: Evil Persists
Book III: Habakkuk's Plea: Elohim Answers

A prophet of God should have answers.... Habakkuk has only questions—questions wrought from sorrow, suffering, and night visions of evil.

When Habakkuk is asked to take in a young refugee—accused of murder—Habakkuk immediately worries about what this will mean for his family of girls. How can he protect them if he brings the enemy under his own roof? But Habakkuk soon discovers an even greater evil residing in the hearts of his kinsmen. Can one man convince a nation to set aside their love of foreign idols and fear the One God alone?

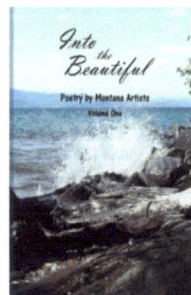

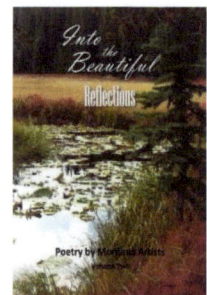

Longing for Rest
A Novella
By S. E. Thomas

One heartbroken woman battles insomnia. Another cannot escape the coma trapping her between dreams and reality. Though they have never met, through a miraculous crossing of consciousness, they find themselves together on a grassy hill surrounded by a mysterious fog. In this dream world, Amy and Gracie form an unusual friendship. But will fear, pain, and betrayal follow them and spoil this haven? Will they finally be able to rest? Can a dream change your life? Available in paperback ($7.99) or eBook ($2.99 from Kindle or Nook.)

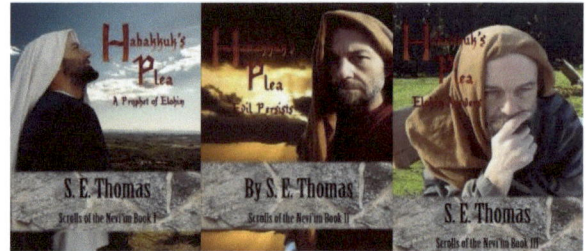

Into the Beautiful
Poetry by Montana Artists
Volumes One & Two

"Into the Beautiful: Poetry by Montana Artists" is a collection of poetry books by Montana artists of all ages. These works of art and creativity were collected through annual contests run August through October. To find out more about this contest, please visit our website at www.thedramaticpen.com.